D1365981

ROTTWEILERS

by Susan H. Gray

Published in the United States of America by The Child's World®
1980 Lookout Drive • Mankato, MN 56003-1705
800-599-READ • www.childsworld.com

PHOTO CREDITS

© Diane Randell/Alamy: 29
© Felipe Rodriguez/Alamy: 23
© Horizon International Images Limited/Alamy: 15
© iStockphoto.com/Eric Isselée: cover, 1
© Mark Raycroft/Minden Pictures: 9, 11, 13, 17, 21, 27
© Stephen Coburn/BigStockPhoto.com: 19
© Steve Skjold/Alamy: 25

ACKNOWLEDGMENTS

The Child's World®: Mary Berendes, Publishing Director;
Katherine Stevenson, Editor

The Design Lab: Kathleen Petelinsek, Design and Page Production

LIBRARY OF CONGRESS CATALOGING-IN-PUBLICATION DATA

Gray, Susan Heinrichs.
  Rottweilers / by Susan H. Gray.
      p. cm. — (Domestic dogs)
  Includes index.
  ISBN 978-1-59296-967-8 (library bound : alk. paper)
  1. Rottweiler dog—Juvenile literature. I. Title. II. Series.
  SF429.R7G73 2008
  636.73—dc22   2007023032

Table of Contents

NAME That DOG!

What dog is named after a city? 🐾 What dog works for the police? 🐾 What dog is as heavy as an eighth-grader? 🐾 What dog is called "Rottie" for short? 🐾 Did you say the Rottweiler (ROT-wy-lur)? 🐾 Then you are right!

5

From Rome to Rottweil

Rottweilers have a long history. They probably came from big, strong dogs that herded cattle. Those dogs lived in Rome over 2,000 years ago. Roman armies marched across Europe. They took cattle with them for food. During the day, the dogs kept the cattle moving. At night, they guarded them.

Years later, people in Europe drove the Romans out. Some of the people lived in a place we now call Germany. These people kept the Romans' dogs. They used them for herding and guarding their own cattle.

The map below shows where Germany and Italy are on Earth. The map on the right shows a closer view. It also shows where the cities of Rottweil and Rome are.

Great Britain

Neth.

Belgium

Lux.

France

Germany

Poland

Lit

Czech

Slovakia

•Rottweil

Switzerland

Austria

Hungary

Italy

Slovenia

Croatia

Romania

Bosnia
And
Herz.

Yugoslavia

Rome

Macedonia

Albania

Greece

Hundreds of years passed. Many German towns sprang up. One of them was called Rottweil. People in Rottweil raised cattle. Their cattle-herding dogs became known as *Rottweiler metzgerhunds* (ROT-wy-lur METZ-ger-hoonts). That means "Rottweil butcher dogs."

In the 1800s, more people began working in factories. Fewer people were raising cattle. Those who did shipped their cattle by train. They no longer needed *Rottweiler metzgerhunds*. The dogs began to disappear.

But some people knew these dogs could do other jobs, too. They put them to work as police dogs and guard dogs. Rottweilers became **popular** again. They are still popular today! In fact, they are one of America's top 20 dog **breeds**.

Many people call Rottweilers "Rotties" for short.

Long ago, Europeans used Rottweilers to pull carts. Later, donkeys took over this job.

These Rottweilers are resting on a porch.

Big, Tough Dogs

Rottweilers are large, strong dogs. They are about 24 inches (61 centimeters) tall at the shoulders. They weigh a little over 100 pounds (45 kilograms). That is about as heavy as an eighth-grader. Some Rottweilers are even bigger.

Rotties have broad heads and powerful jaws. Their noses and lips are black. Their dark brown eyes watch everything around them. These dogs are smart and brave—and they look it!

This alert Rottweiler is watching things across his yard.

Rottweilers' coats have straight hair. It feels hard to the touch. The fur is black with reddish brown markings. The dogs have a brown spot above each eye. They have another brown spot on each cheek. They have more brown around their mouths and on their legs. And they have two brown triangles on their chests.

Rottweilers' bodies are very powerful. Their chests are big, and their legs are strong. These dogs can work for hours without getting tired.

Many Rottweilers have their tails clipped short.

Rottweilers belong to a group of dogs called *working dogs*. These big dogs pull sleds, guard cattle, and act as watchdogs. Great Danes and Saint Bernards are working dogs, too.

You can see that this Rottie's tail was clipped short.

A Loyal Dog

Rottweilers are very **loyal** dogs. They form strong bonds with their owners. They want to **protect** their homes and families. They will accept other people. But first they must know that the people are no danger.

These dogs make good family pets. They love to play with older children. They are not the best choice for homes with small children. They do not understand how big and strong they are. They can easily knock over a small child by mistake.

This Rottweiler is a loved family pet.

Friendly attention is good for Rottweilers. They should get attention from the time they are puppies. That gets them used to being around other people. They can get used to being around other animals, too. Gentle training is good for them. It teaches them how to behave. Then they grow up to be friendly, loving dogs.

Sadly, some owners spend little time with their Rottweilers. They leave them tied up in the yard. They do not pay attention to them. Those things can make a Rottie behave badly. The dog can become mean or hard to control.

Rottweilers need outdoor exercise. They are not good pets for people who live in apartments.

Some owners raise their Rottweilers to be mean and **aggressive**. These dogs can be a danger to people and other animals.

This Rottweiler is being trained to sit and stay.

Rottweiler Puppies

Most Rottweiler mothers have eight to ten puppies in a **litter**. At birth, the puppies weigh almost a pound (one-half kilogram). The pups grow quickly. In the first week, they double their weight. After three weeks, they weigh three times their birth weight!

Newborn Rottweilers' eyes are still closed. Their ears cannot hear yet. They are too weak to lift their heads. They cannot even wag their tails. But in the puppies' first month,

Like all puppies, newborn Rottweilers drink their mother's milk.

all that changes. Their eyes open. Their ears start to hear. They crawl all over their brothers and sisters. They start to play and bite things.

Until now, the puppies have lived on their mother's milk. Now they start wanting other food. They get interested in everything around them, too. They start going farther away from their mother. They play and run around with their brothers and sisters. That helps them learn to get along with other dogs. They learn how to get along with people, too. Soon they will be ready to go to new homes.

The puppies keep on growing—and growing! In their first year, Rottweilers grow quickly. If they play inside, they can knock things over. Owners must keep important things out of the way.

Newborn Rottweilers have ears that stick up. As the pups get older, their ears start to hang down.

These Rottweiler puppies are about six weeks old.

At Home and at Work

Most Rottweiler owners just keep their dogs as pets. They enjoy being around these smart, friendly animals. But many Rottweilers work at other jobs, too.

Some Rotties work as police dogs. They help police officers control large crowds of people. Others help find people who are lost or missing. Some Rottweilers work as guard dogs or watchdogs. They help protect people's buildings or property.

This Rottweiler works as a police dog. He helps officers control crowds at soccer games in Spain.

Rottweilers also make good **service** dogs. They live with people who are deaf, blind, or in wheelchairs. These dogs learn to do lots of things. They turn on lights. They open refrigerators. Some even pull their owners' wheelchairs.

One service dog named Faith became a real hero! One day, Faith's owner was not feeling well. She fell out of her wheelchair. She did not get back up. Faith ran to the phone. She pushed the button that called 9-1-1. When someone answered, Faith barked and barked. The person quickly sent help. When a police officer came, Faith unlocked the door. Help arrived just in time! Faith had saved her owner's life.

Service dogs learn all kinds of things. Many of them know over a hundred **commands**!

This Rottweiler
is a service dog.

Marion Public
1095 6th Avenue
Marion, Iowa 52302-3428
(319) 377-3412

Caring for a Rottweiler

Rottweilers are big dogs that need lots of exercise. They should not stay inside all day. They need to go outdoors and play. Many Rotties love to play catch and go swimming. They enjoy walking and jogging with their owners. Some owners ride bicycles while their Rotties run with them.

A Rottweiler's coat is easy to care for. It should be brushed often with a stiff brush. The dog needs a bath only when it is dirty.

Rottweilers love to play. This Rottie is running in the snow.

Like other large dogs, Rottweilers sometimes have hip problems. Their leg bones do not fit into the hip bones well. The dog might have trouble getting up. It might have trouble walking or running. **Veterinarians** can help treat this problem.

Rottweilers sometimes get a stomach problem called **bloat**. This can happen when the dog eats or drinks too much. The stomach fills with liquid or gas. It hurts a lot! Sometimes the stomach even gets twisted. That can be very dangerous. A dog with bloat needs to see a veterinarian quickly.

Some Rottweilers do have health problems. But most Rotties live healthy lives. With proper care, they can live 12 years or more.

Rottweilers can be messy eaters and drinkers. Some slobber and drool after they eat.

When walking a Rottie outdoors, it is best to use a leash. The dog might see another dog and run off. And even friendly Rotties can easily scare people because of their size.

Does this Rottweiler look as if she is smiling?

29

Glossary

aggressive (uh-GREH-siv) An aggressive animal wants its own way and is ready to attack. Poorly trained Rottweilers can be aggressive.

bloat (BLOHT) When a dog has bloat, its stomach swells and sometimes twists. Rottweilers sometimes get bloat.

breeds (BREEDZ) Breeds are certain types of an animal. Rottweilers are a well-known dog breed.

commands (kuh-MANDZ) Commands are orders to do certain things. Well-trained Rottweilers follow commands.

litter (LIH-tur) A litter is a group of babies born to one animal at the same time. Rottweiler litters often have eight to ten puppies.

loyal (LOY-ul) To be loyal is to be true to something and stand up for it. Rottweilers are loyal to their owners.

popular (PAH-pyuh-lur) When something is popular, it is liked by lots of people. Rottweilers are popular.

protect (pruh-TEKT) To protect something is to keep it safe. Rottweilers protect their homes and families.

service (SUR-viss) Service is work that helps someone. Some Rottweilers work as service dogs.

veterinarians (vet-rih-NAIR-ee-unz) Veterinarians are doctors who take care of animals. Veterinarians are often called "vets" for short.

To Find Out More

Books to Read

American Kennel Club. *The Complete Dog Book for Kids.* New York: Howell Book House, 1996.

Fiedler, Julie. *Rottweilers.* New York: PowerKids Press, 2006.

Gagne, Tammy. *Rottweilers.* Neptune City, NJ: T. F. H. Publications, 2007.

MacPhail, Mary. *Rottweiler.* Buffalo, NY: Firefly Books, 2005.

Pinches, Kate. *Living with a Rottweiler.* Hauppauge, NY: Barron's, 2001.

Stone, Lynn M. *Rottweilers.* Vero Beach, FL: Rourke Publishing, 2005.

Places to Contact

American Kennel Club (AKC) Headquarters
260 Madison Ave, New York, NY 10016
Telephone: 212-696-8200

On the Web

Visit our Web site for lots of links about Rottweilers:

http://www.childsworld.com/links

Note to Parents, Teachers, and Librarians: We routinely check our Web links to make sure they're safe, active sites—so encourage your readers to check them out!

Index

About the Author

Susan H. Gray has a Master's degree in zoology. She has written more than 70 science and reference books for children. She loves to garden and play the piano. Susan lives in Cabot, Arkansas, with her husband Michael and many pets.